CHOOSING
HAPPINESS

CHOOSING HAPPINESS

Lizzie

Lizzie Velasquez

Liguori
LIGUORI, MISSOURI

Imprimi Potest:
Harry Grile, CSsR, Provincial
Denver Province, The Redemptorists

Published by Liguori Publications
Liguori, Missouri 63057

To order, visit Liguori.org or call 800-325-9521

Copyright © 2014 Lizzie Velasquez

All rights reserved. No part of this publication may be reproduced, stored in a retrieval system, or transmitted in any form or by any means—electronic, mechanical, photocopy, recording, or any other—except for brief quotations in printed reviews, without the prior written permission of Liguori Publications.

Library of Congress Cataloging-in-Publication Data

Velasquez, Lizzie.
  Choosing happiness / Lizzie Velasquez.—First Edition.
    pages cm
  ISBN 978-0-7648-2488-3
  1. Happiness—Religious aspects—Christianity. I. Title.
  BV4647.J68V45 2014
  248.4—dc23
                        2014017739

p ISBN 978-0-7648-2488-3
e ISBN 978-0-7648-6936-5

Scripture texts in this work are taken from the *New American Bible,* revised edition © 2010, 1991, 1986, 1970 Confraternity of Christian Doctrine, Washington, D.C., and are used by permission of the copyright owner. All Rights Reserved. No part of the *New American Bible* may be reproduced in any form without permission in writing from the copyright owner.

Liguori Publications, a nonprofit corporation, is an apostolate of the Redemptorists. To learn more about the Redemptorists, visit Redemptorists.com.

Printed in the United States of America
18 17 16 15 14 / 5 4 3 2 1
First Edition

*I dedicate
this book to anyone
who has ever felt trapped,
alone, or hopeless. I want this
book to be the light at the end of
the tunnel. My hope is that you're
able to read this book and feel
ready and excited to choose
happiness above all
else.*

Contents

Foreword

$\mathcal{I}$ have always described myself as an adventure junky. Like a wolf in sheepskin, I've always been a daredevil in a big-haired, big-dimpled, Southern belle's body. My passion for jumping out of airplanes, hiking the most dangerous terrains on earth, swimming with sharks, and volunteering to survive on deserted islands was inevitably a desire to challenge myself and to step outside my comfort zone, most of which I have done with very few fears getting in my way.

That being said, few things have intimidated me as much as when my sweet Lizzie called and asked me to write the foreword to her book. Immediately I was *terrified* that I would do this girl (who I astronomically admire) no justice whatsoever. I was afraid that my words would fail me and only a blank cursor would stare back at me from my computer screen. Yet in the midst of all that insecurity, it dawned on me that THIS is the kind of new frontier, THIS is the crazy adventure (exponentially scarier than any I've ever been on) that Lizzie is daring us to go on. In fact, the *real* daredevil is the person with enough courage to define herself in a world begging for us to conform to everyone else, not the person jumping out of a plane with a perfectly good parachute on her back!

Now, I can't help but reference the first Skype call I ever had with Lizzie. I was in San Fran, she was at home in Austin, and I had read all about her, watched some of her videos online, and (I'm being candid here) was trying my best not to fan-girl her. One of my best friends (Sara Bordo) and I were producing the first TEDxAustinWomen conference, and my job was to convince Lizzie that she wanted to speak at it. I'll spare you the suspense. She said "yes" and gave the talk of her life. In fact, her TEDx talk went viral, and—as I write in April 2014—has more than 9.5 million views!! I'm sure it'll be closer to twenty or a hundred million by the time this book makes it into your hands. I knew I fell in love the moment I met her, but what makes Lizzie so mesmerizing to others?

Among so many things, it's her sense of humor that keeps me fully entertained, her resilience that keeps me in awe, her faith, her grace, and her humility that—when all combined—melts people's hearts. Yeah, Lizzie has a syndrome, blah, blah, blah. The difference is that we could all start our life story with an excuse: an excuse to not live full out, an excuse to not achieve our dreams, an excuse to blame others instead of taking responsibility for our lives. THAT is what Lizzie is here to teach us, to not let others, the world, or even ourselves, label us in ways that don't serve us, in ways that limit us.

I tell people that if the Lord really does place angels among us, then the jig is up, because I already know Lizzie couldn't possibly be human! Lizzie's magnanimity in the face of bullying, in the face of hate, in the face of evil is nothing short of divine. I now (along with Sara) have the privilege to help share her story in a documentary we're making about her life. This book, the last two, and the ten more I'm sure she will write are all here to help guide us to be better humans and to have the courage to turn our adversity and insecurity into our greatest assets and strengths.

Lizzie may be my surrogate baby sister, but she is also my mentor, one of my dearest friends, and a true light bearer on this earth. It is a privilege to say: "That one there, she's mine." It's my honor to watch Lizzie shine, to witness her inspire that same resplendence in others, giving us all permission to be remarkable.

My sweet Lizzie, all BEAUTIFUL you are, there is no flaw in you. It is an honor to be in your corner my dear. I love you so much, and I cannot wait to see what kind of mountains we will move. XO

Alexis Whitney Jones
Founder, I Am That Girl
Author/activist/media personality

Introduction

If someone would have told me a year ago that my second book would be number six on the iTunes top Christian books list, I'd be filmed for major television networks all over the world, I would finally finish my bachelor's degree in communication studies, and I'd start taking the reins of my own career—all by the age of twenty-four—there's no way I would have believed it. If I had been told I would be on a plane with my dearest and best friend headed for the vacation of a lifetime in Maui, Hawaii, I wouldn't have believed it. Sometimes I don't feel worthy of everything that's happening to me. I'm just a girl telling her story, I'm just dorky Lizzie, and I have people telling me I'm their hero. It's like I have two separate lives. In one life I'm just this silly girl who got called names and decided to be happy. In the other life I'm telling other people how to be happy and changing their lives. It's surreal.

But not everything that happened in 2013 was surreal in a good way. If someone had said I'd get a call from my dad on my second day in Hawaii saying my mom was going into septic shock after surgery gone wrong and was being rushed into emergency surgery as we spoke, I—without a doubt—wouldn't have believed it. I wouldn't want to believe that one.

But I can tell you, every single one of those things happened to me. With love, faith, sadness, and confusion, I'm here to tell you yet again that yes—impossible as it seems—all those events happened in 2013.

As some of you may know, I'm no stranger to being put in the position of having to make a decision between two things: choosing happiness or choosing to give up. Living every single day with a syndrome that plenty of people in the world find ugly is something I wouldn't wish on my worst enemy. Luckily, God knew what he was doing when I was born, and he sent me to the two most amazing parents in the world. They unintentionally taught me that no matter what obstacle life puts in front of me, choosing happiness is the only way. Even when I wake up in the morning and I'm dreading having to deal with the ridicule of the outside world, I remind myself of how blessed I am just to have a warm bed to wake up in every morning. How can I wake up grumpy in my big, queen-sized, comfy bed with my little puppy, Bitsy, lying right by my side?

Over the last year, things have happened in my life I never would've expected. Almost losing my mom while I was a seven-hour plane ride away from her was one of the hardest things in the entire world. My family and our faith grew enormously over those months and will continue to grow during the long months of recovery my mom has ahead of her. As a family we've had to really pull together and simply make things work. We had to choose to be happy and to stay strong for our mom because that's what she would do if it were the other way around.

I have learned so many unexpected, difficult, emotionally and mentally draining lessons this past year. But I have also learned that I have grown into a young-adult woman who, despite only weighing about as much as a third-grader, can handle life's obstacles on her own. I know what I deserve and am realizing just what kind of woman I was meant to be. It's been an interesting journey during this past year, on top of an already interesting twenty-four years of life with this...let's just call it "unknown syndrome" for now.

I hope all of the lessons I've learned, the trials I've conquered (or am currently conquering), the growth I've experienced, and the sometimes difficult choices I've had to make can somehow help or relate to you on some level. That's why I wanted to write another book. The obstacles might keep coming, but with a lot of faith in God and myself, I can keep beating them. And you can beat your challenges, too! Not only have I included stories of my own life I hope you can learn from (or laugh at), I've also tried to show that what I've gone through, even though it's individual to me, really is relatable to all of you.

Within each chapter, you'll find activities to strengthen your self-esteem and, hopefully, learn a little more about yourself. At the end of each chapter you'll find reflection questions and some blank space for you to write your answers and also what you learn during your day. There's also room to write your thoughts about my comments—or anything else you want to say—on the "Get Out and Do It" pages. If you need more room to write, go out and get a journal or some blank paper and just keep going!

If there's one thing I've learned as I've grown up, it's that there's always room for change. You don't have to be the person other people tell you to be, you don't have to be the person you were a year ago. Life's a journey we should all enjoy. The destination doesn't matter. Whether you're a reader who's growing up with me, a new reader who picked up the book because you liked the cover, or someone who has gotten this book as a gift, I hope you can use my experiences to gain a little confidence in your own life. Whatever you're going through, wherever you are, there's just one thing I want you to know: You're not alone.

No matter where we come from, what we go through, what language we speak, or what we look like, we all have two choices when faced with any situation.

Will you choose happiness? Or will you choose to give up?

Lizzie Velasquez
September 23, 2013

CHAPTER 1

Growing Up — Finding Joy in the Journey

> *Rather, living the truth in love, we should grow in every way into him who is the head, Christ, from whom the whole body, joined and held together by every supporting ligament with the proper functioning of each part, brings about the body's growth and builds itself up in love.*
>
> EPHESIANS 4:15–16

The Journey to Independence

*The apostles gathered together with Jesus
and reported all they had done and taught.
He said to them, "Come away by yourselves
to a deserted place and rest a while."*
Mark 6:30–31

Filling out college applications, getting recommendation letters, looking up dorm-room décor during my free time, all these things and more consumed my life the second half of my senior year in high school. The thought of having everything be completely different: a change in scenery, new people, a new room—new everything, really—was so exciting to me. I applied to four different colleges. I wanted to get in to all of them, of course, but after being denied by two schools and wait-listed for my top choice, all of my college daydreams started to fade away.

I remember when I received my last letter. The last letter from the last school I applied to. I was standing in the kitchen with my parents. You could feel the anticipation in the air. It took a few minutes of convincing from my mom and dad before I felt ready to open that letter. This was the letter that would decide my fate, my future. I wasn't ready to find out if I was never going to college, or if the fourth time was the charm. The envelope was thick, like it had a packet in it. I took that as a good sign, considering all the other letters I received were just one piece of paper with the words: "Dear Elizabeth, I'm sorry to inform you...."

Once I finally built up the courage to tear open the envelope, I can't tell you how relieved I was to see the words: "Welcome to Texas State!" I don't even remember reading the entire letter! I threw my arms up and started jumping up and down and running around our kitchen. I felt like the world was lifted off my shoulders that instant because I knew I would be going to college! My parents were just as excited as I was. We were all hugging and laughing and enjoying every second of that monumental moment.

Of the four schools I applied to, the only one where I was accepted also happened to be the only one not in Austin. Would I actually be moving away from the house I'd lived in since I was two years old? Would I be able to do it on my own?

Being on your own is scary regardless of what else is going on in your life. Draw a line down the center of a sheet of paper. In the first column, write what scares you about being on your own. In the other, write something you could learn from getting over that fear.

Here's mine:

Doing dishes	My syndrome can't stop me!
Being away from my parents	Coming up with solutions on my own
Being away from my friends	Meeting new friends, trying new things
Failing in college	Challenging myself and learning how I learn
Failing at my career	Finding out ways I can be even better

During the application process, my dad—being the overprotective parent he is—actually offered to pay me to go to school in Austin and stay at home. He said he would pay me every month as long as I lived at home. (I told him he might be late on some payments, and we can't have that! Joking of course….) The offer was tempting, I mean, getting paid just to stay at home! Some people would find that an offer you couldn't pass up. But in the end I knew it wasn't for me. I thanked my dad for his kind (and sneaky) offer, but it was time for me to leave the nest and fly away. Despite needing my parents' help for most of the things in my life because of my syndrome (not to mention being a kid until just recently), I was independent in every aspect of my life that I could be. I was more than eager to take on this next huge chapter of my life, with all the determination and stubbornness I had infused in my little body.

Out of my close group of friends, I was the only one leaving town for college. Granted, I'd only be moving about twenty minutes away, to San Marcos, but it was still going to be a big change for the group of girls who had been attached at the hip since we were eleven years old. Luckily, it wasn't just my friends who were going through the process with me. My cousins, Nikki and Anna, were applying for colleges, too, and (drum roll, please) Anna was accepted to Texas State!

Anna and I were going to be going to the same school! While my family knows I can take care of myself, having Anna at Texas State made them more relieved than anything. Not only would I be going to college with one of my best friends, I'd also have a close relative nearby in case of a medical emergency or anything else bad that might happen. Anna and I decided right away that we wanted to be roommates. We ended up being placed in our top pick, Jackson Hall, right on top of the hill by the student union. Among some of its other features, Jackson Hall has a giant light-up star on the roof that gets lit every time Texas State wins a football game. Now that Anna and I knew we'd be living in our first-choice dorm, all that was left was to wait for move-in day.

The night before I moved to Texas State was unreal, to say the least. All of my clothes, shoes, books, and supplies were packed in brown boxes and clear plastic tubs, not to mention all the memories with my family and best friends I was mentally packing to take with me, too.

I have a confession to make: While we kids were growing up, my parents never really made us do chores. My dad never allowed me to do the dishes because my vision isn't too great, and he was worried I would cut myself. While I normally don't like being told I can't do something because of my syndrome, I milked that one! I mean, there's no way anyone would argue with that rule! Am I right? Now, however, I was thrown into a situation where I not only had to wash my own dishes, but wash them by hand, too!

Not only did I go to college lacking the dishwashing skills I'd need, I also came without knowing another basic task, one that's probably a little more relatable to other college students out there. Laundry. I had no clue where to even begin. In my mind, I was somehow going to both shrink all my clothes and dye everything I owned pink. As if that wasn't intimidating enough, the laundry room in my hall was all the way in the basement. The spooky basement. I felt like I was starring in a scary movie every time I went down there alone.

The first time I did my laundry, I dragged my huge laundry basket downstairs. I called my mom. After hearing her explain to me how to separate by colors, how to use hot and cold water, and all the other details that come with washing clothes, I was over it. I had lost all interest in this part of being on my own. It took almost two hours, and the whole time I stayed in the basement, anxiously awaiting the loud buzzer indicating it was time to take my clothes out. I just knew once that sound went off I was going to open the top of the machine to see all of my clothes ruined. What I did see when I opened the dryer door was something I hadn't imagined. By some miracle, I had successfully done my first load of laundry without ruining anything! I called my mom, sent her pictures, and there might have been a mini-dance party to celebrate my still-intact clean clothes. It's the small victories in life that mean the most.

In addition to doing laundry and washing dishes, there was another practical aspect of living on my own I had to learn to deal with. Due to my bad vision, I've never been able to drive. Having to depend on other people to drive me places has been, and always will be, one of my biggest annoyances in life. I'm independent in so many aspects of my life that it's hard for me to not have control over the driving situation. Just imagine it. Always having to ask and plan ahead anytime you want to go somewhere. Not being able to just pick up and go when you want to. It really takes away the feeling of being free and independent.

Until I went to college, my parents were always the ones who drove me around, but the new friends I made at school all had their own cars, which meant freedom to go wherever we wanted at any time. Going for late-night runs at one in the morning to get tacos made me feel like I was the biggest rebel. My instinct was to tell my parents before I left or let them know when I got back, but now that I was on my own I didn't have to do that. I could just go.

With all this freedom to go where I wanted with my friends and no parents to tell me when it was time to get serious, it took me a few weeks to finally develop a routine. This routine consisted of staying up way too late attempting to do homework, studying, laughing and hanging out with my new friends—and waking up early for class hating myself for staying up so late the night before. Then, somehow, I made it through the day, usually with the aid of lots of coffee or candy. There were some mornings I would have a Reese's and Coke for breakfast. A breakfast of champions, in my opinion.

Besides all of the fun times and laughter with all of my "new college friends," as I called them, the most important reason why I was at school was to further my education. It was very easy to let my newfound freedom take over. I could've easily let having fun take center stage instead of going to class and doing my assignments. It took a lot of discipline and effort to find the right balance between friends, family, resting, and doing well in school.

Choosing to Be Independent

I have been an independent person my whole life. I don't like to be told I can't do something. In fact, I consider that a challenge. Tell me I can't do something and I'll find a way to do it on my own. Even with that daredevil attitude, I was still a little nervous to leave home for college. Everything would be different. The people I relied on wouldn't be so close. My safety net wouldn't be there to catch me immediately if I fell. People wouldn't know my story like they did in high school. I really would be starting all over.

Starting over like that can seem impossible. But if you think about it, we've been taking steps toward independence our whole lives. The older we get, the steps just seem to get a lot bigger. I started kindergarten on my own. I didn't have any friends going there with me. I had to make friends when I got there, and it wasn't easy. I had to reestablish myself in middle school when my friends all split up to go to different schools again. I had to choose different activities to join and hope that I'd make friends when I got there. Then in high school I had to choose what activities to stick with and which ones to drop. I had to start taking steps toward my future career and getting into college. All of those times were scary. But think about the alternative.

What if we never choose independence? What if, instead of joining a club in high school—even though none of your friends are in it—you only do what your friends do? What if you give up on something you like because it isn't what everyone else is doing? What if you pass up the opportunity to go to your dream school because it's too far away from the people you care about? What if you pass on a job because it means you'll have to travel out of your comfort zone?

Saying "no" to all these opportunities doesn't sound like the best choice when you think about it, now does it? Being on your own can be scary when you're starting something new, but that doesn't mean the new thing isn't worth starting. Look back at your list of all the good things that come from getting over your fears. You don't want to miss out on all those things, do you? The best thing that comes from being independent is experience. The experiences may not all be good. In school there were times I missed my family and wanted to go home. There are still times where I'm rushing from one speaking engagement to another where I feel like I just want to give up and hang out with my friends and family, where I don't want to be stressed and rushing all on my own. But I know I have to get past those feelings and do what I need to do. I have a mission and goals. I'd never be able to accomplish any of them if I didn't do things that scared me, things I had to go through alone.

❀ I was nervous, but I did my own laundry.

❀ I was nervous, but I made it through college classes.

❀ I was nervous, but I wrote a book that was published.

❀ I was nervous, but I got in front of people and started speaking.

No one could have done those things for me. I had to embrace what scared me and choose independence. If I didn't, I'd never have made it to where I am right now.

But choosing independence doesn't mean you should be able to do everything on your own all the time. Being independent means knowing where to go for help and being able to ask people for help. It means knowing the difference between being independent and being stubborn. I may have done my own laundry, but I first asked my mom how to start. I graduated from college, but I asked my professors questions and studied with my classmates.

Reflect

In what ways are you already independent?
In what ways are you still growing?

What can you do on your own? What do you need help with?

Think of a time you needed help but didn't feel you could ask.
Why didn't you ask for help?

What are some ways you could start being more independent
but are afraid to try?

Go Out and Do It!

Learning to do my own laundry was really liberating. Find a skill you've always wanted to have and start working toward completion. Whether it's laundry, painting your room, or changing a flat tire, figure out who can help you and then go out and conquer it!

The Journey to a New Me

*Let no one have contempt for your youth,
but set an example for those who believe, in
speech, conduct, love, faith, and purity.*

1 TIMOTHY 4:12

I went into my first week of college classes knowing the number of students in each class was going to be drastically different from what I was used to during my twelve years in elementary, middle, and high school. Going from a class size of twenty-five or less to a classroom of up to 300 students was very intimidating. In middle school and high school, I felt like I was a small fish in an average-size aquarium. In college, I felt like I was a tiny sea horse in a giant ocean. At times I would compare myself to the students who sat in the front row, the students who would answer or ask all the questions and be involved in the discussions during each lecture. The more I compared myself to them the more I thought I wasn't as smart as the other students. Those feelings of self-doubt are enough to make anyone freeze and consider giving up. But I didn't just have inner insecurities to worry about, and the more insecure I felt inside, the more I went back to my other, less confident self on the outside.

When I was in first grade, I was given my first monocular. It's like a pocket-size binocular, but it's only one small tube. I had to use it to help me see the board clearly from wherever I was sitting in the classroom. All of my friends thought my monocular was cool, but I wasn't a fan of it for many years. With lots of practice, the monocular became more and more helpful, and I became very dependent on the little guy. I could focus it, keep up with the teacher, and oftentimes hold it in a way that you couldn't even tell I was using it. When I got to college, the classrooms were in large lecture halls that put me even farther away from the teacher and the board. This would have been the perfect time for me to use the monocular, but I started to revert back to when I first got it. I was too embarrassed to use it during class. I felt like I stood out like a sore thumb enough, and I didn't want to draw any more attention to myself than necessary. Because I stubbornly refused to use my monocular, I had to suffer the consequences of messing up my notes and getting lots of migraines from eyestrain trying to see the board. All in hopes of looking "cool."

Eventually my stubbornness against using the monocular started affecting my grades negatively. I knew I had to bite the bullet and start using it again. After not using it for so long, it took a while to adjust. It wasn't fun having to readjust to using the monocular, but I'm so glad I did. If I hadn't given in, I'd have spent the rest of college having a hard time, getting migraines, and not learning anything. Besides, after I started using my monocular, no one in class stopped to tell me I looked lame or stupid.

This wasn't the only way I had to move out of my comfort zone either. Because of my syndrome, I have a very weak immune system, which means I had an excuse to have unlimited absences each semester. In college, some professors decide you can only have three absences per semester or it brings your final grade down. I had a letter that explained my situation, and I had to have it signed by each of my professors and turn it back into the Office of Disability on campus. Initially it felt awkward going to my professors to have them sign that piece of paper; just another way I had to be different. However, it actually turned into something that really helped me. Being in such large classes, it's sometimes hard for professors to have a one-on-one connection with every student. Since I had to get my letter signed the first day of class,

I would wait until the lecture was over, go up to the teacher, and introduce myself. I would always put on my friendliest smile, explain my situation, and make sure to let the professor know that I was looking forward to the course. It not only established a connection, but it gave me a sense of belonging.

Choosing to Grow Up

While all these situations eventually worked themselves out, it was intimidating to have to learn to be comfortable in my own skin again. Through all the challenges I've had because of my syndrome, I've learned new ways to look at things. I'm appreciative of every moment I have, and I know everything I've gone through—or will have to go through—is a learning tool, a ladder that keeps me moving higher. That doesn't mean these obstacles are ever easy. It doesn't mean I never get annoyed with people staring at me or feel self-conscious about the way I look. Every new situation gives me another chance to overcome the labels, my appearance, and let people see me for who I am.

But who exactly is Lizzie? That question isn't as easy to answer as you might think.

In middle school, I really wanted to be a cheerleader, but not because I was athletic or had a passion for cheering. I just wanted the outfit. Partly because it was cute, but also because wearing that uniform meant I was part of something. It meant I fit in. I did end up making the varsity cheerleading team in middle school (so did every other person who tried out), and I thought that meant I fit in. If I dressed like everyone else, I felt I would look like everyone else. But that didn't happen. I had a lot of fun on the cheerleading team, but I also started to realize there were always going to be people who singled me out because of the way I looked. I had to make a choice, even at this young age, about whether I wanted to be miserable or happy.

I really did try to be happy. I put on a happy face at school and at home with my parents, anywhere people could see me. But at night, when I was taking a bath and getting ready for bed, I would cry. I'd let out all those emotions I tried to hide because I knew no one could see me. I'd plead with God, hoping that if I just scrubbed hard enough he'd wash my syndrome away, and I'd look in the mirror and see a normal face. That never happened. I was mad at God for a long time because of that, and in those moments—trust me—choosing happiness was not easy. In fact, some days it wasn't a choice I could make.

At that point in my life, I was dark, moody, teenage Lizzie. I was mad at the world and didn't know how to get better. But I knew that wasn't the person I wanted to be. That wasn't the Lizzie I wanted people to know me as. It wasn't the destination I wanted to end up at. So I started to listen to my friends and family and began to come to terms with who I was. Little by little, I started to tell God that if he wasn't going to make me pretty, then he had to show me why I had this syndrome and what good I was supposed to be doing.

Then I got to high school and found "that video" and felt like all the growing up I'd done went away. I wasn't as strong or as confident as I thought. I was still scared, insecure, and not only did I want to give up but I wanted to hurt other people the way I was hurting. This was another stage of my journey where I had to make a choice. I could turn into someone with more in common with my bullies than myself or I could find a way to rise above the pain. I could prove I wasn't what they said I was and do it in a way that was true to the person I wanted to be. It wasn't easy, but choosing happiness doesn't always mean choosing the easy route.

Not too long after that, I started speaking, and things started to fall into place. God's plan started to make sense. I finally started to accept that this was who I was, and that happy person was who I wanted to be. I started to like myself. I started to love myself. I started to be proud of who I was and what I looked like. I realized I actually could be comfortable in my own skin.

There are still days I have doubts and feel self-conscious, like using the monocle in my college classes or being afraid I won't be able to live on my own without my family support system. But I finally have an idea of who I'm capable of being, and to be that person I sometimes have to be brave. The older I get, the more I realize I have to take control of my own personality and my own definition of myself. My life was (and is) in my hands, just like your life is in your hands. You're the driver. You decide whether you go down a good path or a bad path. I decided to turn every hateful, nasty comment and stare into fuel to keep me working even harder and to look at every challenge as a new opportunity. You have the same choice.

Once I made that choice, everything else started to fall into place. I knew I wanted to go beyond what everyone else in the world thought of me and my appearance. I knew my mission was to get my story out there, to let people know you don't need to let your appearance or other people's negativity stop you. I knew I wanted to be a motivational speaker and help other people learn from my experiences. I wanted to be an author and a college graduate as well. Some day I want to have my own family and expand my career even further. But I don't want to be limited by just one label. I wanted to have them all, because we're all more than just one label. We are more than just what we're told we're good or bad at. We're more than our appearance, more than our limitations, more than our fears.

There are lots of things I want to be and accomplish in my life, kind of like a personality bucket list of all the things I want to do or be. Take a minute and create one of your own. List all the things you've been and all the things you want to be in the future, and put a check mark by the things you've already accomplished. Don't limit yourself or worry that you can't do everything. You never know where life is going to take you, so don't limit the journey!

Lizzie's **Personality Bucket List**

- ☑ Cheerleader
- ☑ Writer
- ☑ Motivational speaker
- ☑ Daughter
- ☑ Friend
- ☑ Forgiver
- ☑ Optimist
- ☑ College graduate
- ☐ Founder of my own company
- ☐ Web designer
- ☐ Computer guru
- ☐ Wife
- ☐ Mother

Figuring out who we are, or "growing up," is an ongoing process. We'll always be challenged and have bad days when we want to give up. The important thing is that we must never give in to those voices that tell us we can't, whether those voices are from the outside or inside our own hearts. If there's something you want to do, you can find a way to do it. Sometimes all it takes is being brave enough to start.

Reflect

What is your mission in life?

What do you know you want to do in the future?
(Or, what don't you want to do?)

What does it mean to you to be successful in your life?

How do you want other people to see you?

Go Out and Do It!

In the next few weeks (it doesn't have to be today), say "yes" to an opportunity you'd normally say "no" to and see what happens. If you're nervous, say a prayer or bring a friend, but don't give up. If you love it, great! If you hate it, find a way to use the experience to grow.

CHAPTER 2

Life as a Motivational Speaker — Inspiring Change

No foul language should come out of your mouths, but only such as is good for needed edification, that it may impart grace to those who hear.

EPHESIANS 4:29

How I Got My Start

> *Therefore, putting away falsehood, speak the truth, each one to his neighbor, for we are members one of another.*
> EPHESIANS 4:25

*I*f you haven't been paying attention to the Bible quotes at the beginning of each section (I know some of you just skip over them!), take a look at the two at the start of this chapter. They come from a section of Ephesians titled "Rules for the New Life" in the *New American Bible*. They have a lot of meaning if you're a Catholic like me, but I'd like to think of them right now as rules for starting over. The basic idea of this section of Ephesians is that we should all be nice to each other, only saying kind and truthful things. That's the message I try to get across when I speak, because I know more than most people what it means to have to start over.

I started motivational speaking when my assistant principal asked if I would be willing to give a speech to 400 freshmen at my high school. Of course my first response was, "NO!" I didn't want to go in front of all those people! I didn't know what I'd say. I thought I'd be really boring, and none of the other kids would be able to relate to me. For some reason, though, I decided to do it anyway. I planned out what I was going to say, wrote notes so I wouldn't forget a word, and found the confidence to go up on stage. What happened next was what made me decide to change my plans and do this for a living. For the longest time, I thought no one would be able to relate to me at all. No one (well, two other people) has my syndrome or knows what it's like to walk in my shoes. But after giving that speech, I realized all these people really *could* relate to at least something I'd been through. Whether it was bullying, a lack of self-confidence, or learning to forgive others, I could connect with them about something. I felt excited and proud that I could be a resource for them. I realized I really could reach people with my story, and I knew that if I could just make a difference in one person's life, I had to do it.

After realizing public speaking was actually a job you could get paid for, I knew the pieces of my puzzle were coming together. God was guiding me down the path he'd had in mind for me all along. I had no clue what I would need to learn to be professional speaker, I didn't know how to let people know I was available to speak, I didn't know if it looked professional to go in front of people with notes or if I should memorize things. So that's when the research started. I sat in front of my laptop, looked for "how to be a motivational speaker," and started researching. I made lists of everything I needed to do:

- ❀ Make a website so people will know how to contact me for speaking engagements.

- ❀ Get a professional email address, probably something that doesn't have the words "cheer baby" in it.

- ❀ Make a list of topics I am both qualified to speak on and interested in talking about.

- ❀ Decide what kind of audiences I want to speak to.

My next step was to study the way other people speak. I used my dad as my first example because as a teacher, principal, and religious instructor he'd had a lot of experience talking in front of people. I watched how often he'd walk around or how long he'd stand in the same spot, and I took notes about when he made jokes and when his personality would come through. I watched how the audience would react to him and how he'd speak to different groups of people. I soaked everything up like a sponge and was always ready to learn more.

Once I felt confident in my ability, I made a website and started emailing local schools, churches, and businesses in my area to let them know who I was in case they were looking for a speaker. My first real speaking engagement was for a teen retreat my aunt was leading through her church. I would have to prepare thirty minutes of material. THIRTY MINUTES OF MATERIAL?! I'd never had to fill that much time before! I was a first-time speaker! How would I ever be able to talk that long? I started writing down my speech word for word only to realize that was just making me even more nervous. I knew what I wanted my message to be, I knew the kind of audience I was going to have, and I wanted to be able to get in front of them and know I was speaking from my heart. So I tossed the written speech and settled for four bullet points I could memorize. The rest was up to God.

Choosing Where to Go Next

Over the next couple of years, I repeated this same process. I started out my career just doing a couple of speeches a month, sometimes to groups as small as four people! But all I really cared about was the experience. Whatever career you feel called to—whether it's speaking, teaching, computer programming, sales, or whatever—you can't really learn it unless you're willing to dive in and get your hands dirty.

Tips for Accomplishing a Goal

Whether you're hoping to start your dream career, get into a top college, finish a school project, or just complete a personal goal, it can be intimidating to figure out where to start, so here are a few tips to get you started.

1. **What do you want to do?**

   This sounds like a simple step, but figuring out your exact goal is an important starting place. Write it down somewhere so you remember. If you want, you can include why this goal is so important to you as a way to keep you motivated.

2. **What do you need to get there?**

   If your goal is getting into a top college, figure out what the entrance requirements are. If your goal is finishing a project for class, what do you need to make it happen? If it's a personal goal to learn how to dance or do rock climbing, what equipment will you need to get started?

3. **Who should you ask for help?**

   Is there a teacher, parent, friend, or instructor you can ask for help? If you're starting your dream career, can you job-shadow someone and use that person as a mentor? Can you ask your teacher to mentor you, proofread your essays, or write letters of recommendation?

4. **Make a plan to start.**

   Deciding to do something is one thing. Actually doing it is the scary part. Make your list like I did when I decided to become a motivational speaker. What do you need to do to get started, and when are you going to do it? If you're really organized, make a timeline, too.

Sometimes I'd give speeches where the people in the audience would spend most of the time looking down at their phones. I'd start to wonder if I was boring, rambling, or just pretending that speaking was what I was supposed to do. I had days where I just wanted to give up. But I didn't. I chose to be happy, to see every bored audience member as an opportunity to improve. They weren't insulting me, they were helping me become better. I didn't have to let them make me angry. Once I made that choice, I started to get better. Speaking requests started picking up so quickly I couldn't keep up with them, and I had to enlist family members to help out as part of Team Lizzie. Before each speech, I would find a place where I could be alone to pray. I would pray for God to put his hands over me, keep me calm, and help the words that came out of my mouth be his. Giving up is an easy choice when we think we're failing. It takes a lot of courage to choose to keep moving forward and trust that, as long as you're willing to work for it, things will get better.

Even though things were going well and my motivational speaking career—my dream job!—was going better than I imagined, there were times I'd find myself complaining about all the traveling and how rundown I felt. Every time I received a speaking request, I would immediately say "yes" because I couldn't bring myself to say "no." I was still in college, still trying to have a normal college experience and social life, and I missed my regular routine back home. I found myself contemplating whether or not this was what God wanted me to do. Yes, I was speaking and sharing his message, but I was also worn down. I just wanted to hang out with my friends.

When We Doubt Ourselves

I'm sure most of you reading this aren't motivational speakers or would even want to be, but that feeling of being overwhelmed and rundown can happen to anyone, no matter whether you're working full time, part time, or still a student. We get so caught up in being better and better, taking on more and more, that we start losing sight of what's all around us. If you're working to get into a good college, you might be taking so many college-credit courses in high school that you don't have time to actually enjoy your time there. Or you might be like me, working so hard to get your dream career off the ground that you don't get to enjoy the journey. Or maybe you're working multiple jobs just to survive, without an opportunity to just sit and enjoy being alive.

Sometimes these times are unavoidable. Sometimes we have no choice but to be stressed and overbooked. We offer it up to God and move on. But we can't live like that forever. I know because I've tried. I hate having to take time off. I feel like I'm missing something or that I'm letting people down, whether it's my fans, my family, or myself. I think, *if I can just keep going, everything will work out.* Luckily, I have doctors who tell me I have to take time off, whether I like it or not. It's hard to take time off and unplug... but it's worth it!

As much as I love speaking and being busy, there's something about taking time for myself that's even better. Being able to get up and start the day with a cup of coffee and a book is one of the best feelings. Being able to take a step back and spend some time appreciating where I started and where I am now makes me grateful and keeps me from taking things for granted. And maybe most important of all, it helps me recharge. When we keep forcing ourselves ahead with no time to relax, we'll eventually collapse, and that isn't good for anyone.

Signs You Need to Stop and Recharge

❅ You're always exhausted but never have time to sleep.

❅ You get irrationally upset about little things.

❅ You start to snap at people for no reason.

❅ The only free time you have is when you occasionally sleep and eat.

❅ You're praying for the day your goals are complete so you can relax.

❅ All you see is the destination; enjoying the journey no longer seems important.

There's one other thing that keeps me going when I feel so overwhelmed I want to give up: all of you. Those times in the airport when I was questioning whether or not this is what I wanted to do? I started going through my emails. When I started, I was almost in tears because I was so tired. I felt like I was at my wits' end. After sorting through spam and work-related messages, I read a letter from a girl all the way in New Zealand. In her email she said we would more than likely never meet in person, but she wanted to thank me for doing what I was doing. She said the courage I had to tell people it's OK to be different and it's OK to stand your ground and be true to yourself helped her so much she wanted to encourage me to keep doing it.

I have people tell me this all the time. I don't always have time to reply to everyone, but I read every message, and when I do I get the strength to keep going. It helps me open my eyes to all the blessings right in front of me.

Reflect

What do you feel you're called to do?

What's your plan for making it happen?
(If you don't have one, start one here!)

Do you have times when you feel overwhelmed?
How do you handle it?

What activities or people help you recharge?

Go Out and Do it!

Make a list of all the things you enjoy doing but don't feel you have time for. Then find time to do at least one of those things every week. If you can, try to make time to do one of those things every day.

Not Done Yet!

> For I am the LORD, your God, who grasp your
> right hand; It is I who say to you, Do not fear, I
> will help you.
>
> ISAIAH 41:13

You would think that after years of motivational speaking I'd never get nervous on a stage, but that's not true at all! In 2012, I was asked to speak to my largest audience ever at the Boston STAND UP TO BULLYING rally. When I got there, the production assistant asked if I wanted to see the stage where I'd be speaking. Unknowingly, I walked into the arena and was told that over 5,000 students and teachers would be attending that day. My mom and I just stood there without saying anything. A million feelings and thoughts were running through my head. This was what I wanted, to speak to the masses and spread my message. My dream was coming true. My mom had tears rolling down her face. We just looked at each other and knew we were thinking the same thing: God is good.

We went back to our waiting area, and that was when the shock set in. Was I really going to speak in front of 5,000 people about my story? Could I actually do this? I only had ten minutes to talk. How could I fit everything I needed to say into ten minutes? To get my mind off things, we walked around and looked at the different booths that were set up. I walked past a booth with my picture and a table filled with my book *Be Beautiful, Be You.* It felt like a dream. A lady and her son were working at the table with my books. She asked me if I was nervous. I was shaking in my boots. The lady picked up a small, clear rock with an angel inside it. She told me to hold the angel rock in my hand until I spoke, and God would be with me and the angel would take away my nervousness. I carried the rock in my hand and never let go. I didn't even realize I was still holding it until I started walking on stage and quickly stowed it in my pocket.

I got on stage, held the microphone up to my mouth, and just started talking. All the nerves and doubts were gone. I felt like I was talking to 5,000 of my best, closest friends. I forgot I only had ten minutes to speak (they had a sign to let me know when five minutes were up, but the person held it on my right side—my blind side—so I couldn't see it). I wrapped up my speech when it felt right, which ended up being exactly ten minutes. I knew it was my angel rock. It's amazing how much a small gesture like that can mean.

Ever since then I have that angel rock with me somewhere any time I give a speech. I'll always be grateful to that woman in Boston who gave me this pocket-sized angel. Sometimes I hold that angel rock even when I'm not speaking. When I'm nervous about traveling or organizing plans on my own, I hold my angel rock and pray for help.

Choosing Strength

When I was growing up, my parents always told me God knew our exact path in life (even the wrong turns). He knows what we are meant to do and who we are meant to be. I had to stop asking "why?" and start listening to what God says. While my professional experience is limited to inspirational writing and motivational speaking, I've learned three things that have helped me in more circumstances than those. I hope they'll also help you overcome whatever fears you need to overcome.

Relax.

Worrying and making yourself anxious about something isn't going to help. Talk yourself up, be confident in who you are and what you're going to do. People respond to you when you're confident (even if you're just faking it). If you make a mistake, that's OK. People understand.

Keep It Simple.

Whatever you're doing, when other people are involved it's best to keep things simple. Don't overcomplicate things for yourself because it'll just trip you up and give you more to worry about, and other people will appreciate a message they can follow from start to finish.

Trust Yourself.

Even if you're trying something for the first time, know that you'll do the best you can. You can be miserable about every new experience or scary situation, or you can be grateful for the opportunity. Messing up isn't failure. It's a learning experience.

Speaking to middle-school students

My brother, Chris, and sister, Marina

Individual photos of Lizzie were taken by Ryan Towe Photography, Des Moines, IA

With Bobby Bones on his nationally syndicated radio show

Vacationing with my family

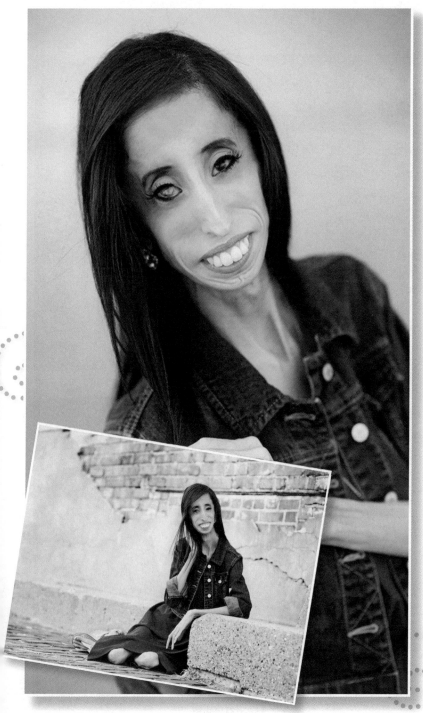

Filming a TV documentary

Hanging out with fans

*Barbara Walters on the set of
The View*

The View's Whoopi Goldberg

The View's
Sherri Shepherd

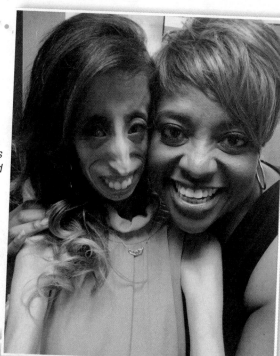

The View's *Jenny McCarthy*

Entrepreneur Bill Rancic

th Marie Osmond after my speech
Paul Mitchell School in Las Vegas

During my TEDxAustin speech

Dr. Drew Pinsky and Mom

On camera during interviews

On the E! *set*

On the set of a TV documentary

Speaking to junior-high students in Gonzales, TX

On the set of a TV documentary with, from left, Ngoc Nguyen, Sara Bordo, and Alexis Jones

Sara Bordo
DIRECTOR

I like speaking for the adrenaline rush I get when I'm up on stage. It's like therapy for me. I can talk candidly in a room of strangers and know they won't judge me because I'm explaining myself and I'm being honest, even if I'm nervous that I'll forget something or worried about doing a good job. I love going into a room to talk to people who've never heard of me before. I used to get upset when people would judge me by appearance or talk to my parents, assuming I can't speak for myself. But now those experiences drive me. I know that once I talk, at least one person in the audience will be able to relate to what I have to say. That makes everything worthwhile.

When I gave my TEDxAustinWomen talk in 2013, I planned for weeks. I took notes and outlined everything I was going to say. I didn't want to embarrass myself in front of all those professional women. I was the closing speaker of the day. After listening to incredible speakers share their innovative thoughts and ideas, I realized that everything I listened to throughout the entire day was crucial for me to include in my speech. I put myself in a position where I had to decide to either trust my instincts or stick with what I had planned. Luckily, I went with my gut. So I ditched the notes and decided to just go on stage and talk. When I got on stage, a group of high-school girls was on the floor in front of the stage with pillows and blankets, looking casual and relaxed. I could interact with them better than the rest of the audience, so I focused on them and just started talking. That helped me bond with the whole audience, and when I was done I was overwhelmed with gratitude. This wasn't the perfect speech I planned and rehearsed, it was just me. Being just Lizzie was enough. The audience and everyone who watched the video later were inspired by me just being me. We later found out that out of all of the TEDWomen conferences across the nation that day, the TEDxAustin event was the number one most-viewed, and I was part of that!

I'm not even sure how to describe that feeling. I have gone from a girl who wanted to scrub away her skin to one who is so confident in who she is, I'm inspiring other people to love themselves for who they are. If there's one thing I want you to take away from this section, it's that you have something to offer the world, too. It might not be the same thing I have, or your friends have, or your parents and family members have, but that's the way it's supposed to be. You're not supposed to offer the world the exact same thing as someone else. You're supposed to be uniquely you, and once you find that thing you love, be willing to share it with the world, even if you start off feeling vulnerable. That feeling of knowing you're accepted as who you are, that you can inspire people just by being you, that you're worth being loved and listened to even if you're not perfect is worth it. Don't ever be afraid to become the best version of yourself.

I hated God for making me with this syndrome I can't change. I'm sure you've had days when you've hated God or the universe for something you can't change. That's OK. That's normal. But don't let those feelings limit you or run your life. Take what makes you different and find a way to use it. Give people the chance to accept you for who you are, as you are.

Go find your "angel rock" (or whatever it may be) and use it to help you conquer your fears. All people have something they're afraid to do, whether it's a new job or school you don't think you can conquer, or something you've always wanted to do but been too afraid to try. Know that God has your plan already set. He's just waiting for you to make that first step, and let him take it from there. I know I'm not done doing things that scare me. I know I'm going to have to stay strong and keep building on what I already have, but I'm ready to keep going.

Reflect

Make a list of the things that scare you.

What about these things scare you?

Now make a list of things you can do to tackle those fears head-on.

What do you feel now? (It's OK to still be afraid!)

Go Out and Live It!

Sometimes we need another person to help us overcome our fears. Keep an eye out for the chance to be somebody else's angel rock. Whether it's giving a friend a pep talk before a presentation or leaving an encouraging comment on someone's blog or video. Even something that little can make a difference. Let someone else know: You're not alone.

CHAPTER 3

Bullying — How Do You Define Yourself?

> Be strong and steadfast; have no fear or dread of them, for it is the LORD, your God, who marches with you; he will never fail you or forsake you.
>
> DEUTERONOMY 31:6

> *Do to others whatever you would have them do to you. This is the law and the prophets.*
>
> MATTHEW 7:12

The girl who has to eat every fifteen minutes.

THE WORLD'S SKINNIEST WOMAN.

The world's ugliest woman.

Skinny bones.

Freak.

Monster.

It.

he labels on the opposite page are the labels the world handed to me. If you've ever been bullied, you have a list of your own. These labels are what we feel society thinks we're worth. The longer we hear them, the more we start to think that's what we're worth. It's a hard mindset to overcome. It's the kind of thing we can carry for the rest of our lives.

My Story

Growing up, I didn't know my syndrome made me look different. My parents treated me normally. My family treated me normally. My friends treated me normally. It was when I started kindergarten that the harsh reality of the "real world" hit me. That's a pretty big slap in the face for a five-year-old.

I was pumped for my first day of kindergarten! I was ready to take on the world! I was grown up! Then I got to school. I saw a girl playing by herself, so I went up to play with her. She just stared at me. She was scared of me.

I decided that was just her problem. More blocks (or whatever we were playing with) for me. Then it was time for recess. I went with the rest of the kids to play on the slide. I'd been looking forward to going down that slide all day! All the other kids moved away from me. I thought it was because I was special. I thought I was the new slide VIP! It took a few more days for it to finally sink in. Something was wrong with me. The other kids didn't think I was normal. They moved away because they were scared of me. Not because I was special.

I eventually made it through elementary school. I made some friends who vouched for me to the other kids, but the older I got, the worse it got. In middle school, I would wait in line, doing what I was supposed to, just to have other kids walk by and laugh or point me out to their friends and whisper. The name-calling started after that. I couldn't go to theme parks or Chuck E. Cheese's like the rest of my family because people would just stare. It wasn't just little kids, either. Little kids always stare at things that are different or that they haven't seen before, but adults would stare, too. People I'd never met before would ask my parents why they didn't feed me. Doctors would ask what eating disorder I had without even looking at my medical history.

I started to get depressed. I was more moody than a thirteen-year-old girl should be. I was mad at God. I was mad at the world. I wanted to show the world it was wrong, but no one wanted to give me that chance. Then I got to high school. Then I found "that video." That video was eight seconds long. It just showed me. It had millions of views and thousands of comments. It was titled *The World's Ugliest Woman.*

I read every comment. None was positive. I didn't want to tell my parents because I didn't want them to get hurt, too. I had a habit of crying in the bathtub where no one could see me, and I hid it like that for a while.

Finally I got the courage to tell my parents. We tried to get the video taken down, but the person who posted it refused. He said he'd keep posting it no matter what, that he'd make sure that video followed me around. He said he'd never stop. I wondered why I was trying so hard to be myself if I was just going to be made fun of anyway. I wanted to hit my keyboard and fight back. I thought about becoming a bully myself.

But I didn't.

Choose to Keep Going

If you've been bullied, you know that feeling of just wanting to give up. You've already fought and lost. You won't be able to change other people's minds. Might as well just accept this is the way it is. I've been to that place. I almost gave in.

Then a thought came to me. Who was I going to let define me? My goals and accomplishments? Or the people who only wanted to define me by my appearance? Sure, there were days I prayed to look normal. I wanted to be able to go in the bathroom and scrub off my syndrome, to just be normal. But that wasn't going to happen.

And that was OK.

I finally realized I was more than my syndrome. I was going to take the worst experience of my life and find a way to make it a positive. I would fight back with my accomplishments. I prayed to God, saying that if he gave me this syndrome for a reason he'd show me what I was supposed to do. That's when I started speaking and reaching out to other people who have been bullied like me. I knew I wanted to use my experiences to help other people through theirs.

It can be hard to keep going after something devastates you like that video devastated me. It's easy to say, "tough it out" and "things will get better." They will, but you'll still struggle. Just remember, you can't fully enjoy your life and your purpose until you love yourself. It wasn't until I was confident in who I was that things started to fall into place. In *Be Beautiful, Be You*, I ask for you to make a list of all the things you love about yourself. If you have one, great! If you don't, make one. Hang it up where you can see it. But don't let that list define you, either. I am more than just my awesome hair, even though I love it. Even good labels or neutral labels can hold us back from where we're supposed to go.

Let's say you're a self-proclaimed bookworm. You love to read. You're proud of it. All your friends ask you for book recommendations. It's part of who you are. Does that mean you can't also like music? Or volleyball? Or astrophysics? Or that you can't decide you want to binge-watch TV for a week and not pick up a book? No.

What if you've labeled yourself a jock? You love sports. Maybe you're even planning to get a scholarship to play in college. Does that mean you can't also be on the debate team? Or write poems for the literary magazine? Or have friends who aren't athletic? No!

We're all more than just what we, or the people around us, have labeled us. And we're all allowed to change and grow. Would you want to eat at a restaurant that only had one thing on the menu? Or would you want options and variety? If your answer is "yes," then don't limit yourself to a side dish. You're a whole meal, with multiple courses and a variety of side dishes, and you can always add more as you go.

Write down a list of everything you've ever been labeled. Then cross out those names and write your name.

Lizzie's label list:

~~The World's Ugliest Woman~~	**Lizzie**
~~Freak~~	**Lizzie**
~~Motivational Speaker~~	**Lizzie**
~~Cheerleader~~	**Lizzie**
~~Catholic~~	**Lizzie**
~~YouTube celebrity~~	**Lizzie**

Your label list:

_____   _____

_____   _____

_____   _____

_____   _____

_____   _____

_____   _____

_____   _____

_____   _____

_____   _____

_____   _____

These labels might describe things you do or believe. Some of them might be positive. Some of them might show what you've had to overcome. But none sums up everything it means to be you. As much as I'd like to get rid of all labels, I know that's probably not going to happen. I also can't control the labels people assign me.

I would love to see an article about me that doesn't have "the world's ugliest woman" label in it anywhere. That's not something I really want to be synonymous with my name, but I know it's an attention-getter. I may not like it, but it's one way to draw people in, get them interested, and make them listen. If I had to go through something bad every day, I would, just to show everyone else who's been labeled and bullied that it really is possible to get through it and turn it into a positive. It's possible for things to get better as long as you don't give up. My labels might not be able to choose happiness on their own, but who I am—Lizzie Velasquez—can choose to be happy as every one of those things, from successful speaker to world's ugliest woman.

Reflect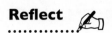

Think of an experience you've had with bullying (yourself or someone else). How did it make you feel?

What (or who) do you stay strong for?

What's something you've wanted to do but felt like you couldn't because of your labels?

What kind of person do you want to be?

Go Out and Do It!

The next time you see someone you think you know but have never really talked to, listen to what that person has to say. Don't let what you've heard about the individual influence your opinion. Let that person show you who he or she is.

Choosing to Stop Before You Start

> *Take no revenge and cherish no grudge*
> *against your own people. You shall love*
> *your neighbor as yourself. I am the LORD.*
> LEVITICUS 19:18

It took a long time for me to finally overcome bullying. I still deal with it even now. Not everyone who comments on my YouTube videos or sends me an email is doing it to be kind and supportive. The bullying will never stop. Being able to joke about everything has been a struggle. I started my life not even knowing there was such a thing as bullying, and now I know it's an everyday reality of my life.

While writing this book, I became aware of a new trend on the internet, one that's almost crueler than "that video." People would video themselves looking at online pictures of me and then make faces, pretend to throw up, scream, every mean and disrespectful thing you can think of. Then they'd post the videos online. If you're thinking I should be used to this by now, should just ignore it, unplug from the internet and not watch it, it's not that easy. Things like that aren't things you can just shake off. But that trend isn't why I bring this story up.

I have a lot of fans, and I love every one of them. They are the reasons I do what I do. They are the people who make all this work worth it. It's nice to know I have a community of people behind me, and when I started to get harassed by a few ignorant people, my fans rose up in my defense by bullying the bullies. I am grateful to have so many people willing to come to my defense, but bullying for any reason is wrong. We're better than that! We should support each other, not sink to the bullying level. Being kind to the people who hurt you is harder than just living with their hateful comments, but that's how we show we're stronger. Fighting back with our accomplishments, our success, our prayers, and our support is the only kind of fight I'm willing to get behind.

But it shouldn't even get to that point. We should be fighting for a culture that doesn't foster bullying at all.

What We Can Do

So how do we start?

1. **You don't have to have a syndrome for people to be nice to you.** My syndrome has been a blessing because it has enabled me to do what I love and make a difference in people's lives, but a lot of people outside the limelight are being bullied, and they need support, too. I don't want my followers to just rally around me, I want them to rally around each other. Every one of us is worthy of kind words, of people to come to our defense and let us know bullying is wrong. I'd love to see my followers, viewers, and readers go out and tell the kid who always sits alone, gets picked last, is talked about online that "you are loved," "you are worth more than this." Everyone has a story. Take the time to learn it.

2. **Be courageous enough to talk.** When we talk about differences or diversity, it's usually discussed in vague terms. It's something we all know about but don't risk discussing because that conversation might be uncomfortable. But I say, talk about

it! Get everything out in the open. Let's start discussing what makes us different and what we can learn from each other. On the first day of school every year, my dad and I would go into my classroom and talk to my classmates about my syndrome and explain why I look so different. I was open to questions, answered them head-on, and then everyone just moved on. There was nothing to whisper about because I was not a secret.

3. **Put things in perspective.** I'm blind in my right eye. That used to bother me. Then I went to my first conference for the visually impaired. We all had nametags in a font so large you could read them all from the back of the room, with our names in braille underneath that. Because I can see out of my left eye, I was able to read everyone's name and went up to a group of people my age and called them by name. One of the people in the group spoke up first: "Oh, you can see." "Only out of one eye!" was my immediate response. But that's the first time I've ever thought of it as being blind in only one eye. I could still see. I was blessed. Sometimes all it takes is the ability to think about a negative thing in a positive way.

4. **Surround yourself with positive people and good influences.** Whether you're being bullied or on the sidelines, the people you choose to surround yourself with are going to determine how you respond. If you have people around you who feel good only when putting other people down, you're probably going to bully someone, whether you realize it or not. If you surround yourself with good, positive people, you're going to have a stronger foundation. If it weren't for my friends, my family, and my faith, getting to where I am today would have been a lot harder. It might not have been possible at all.

5. Set the bar higher. Don't settle for what other people tell you that you deserve. I like it when people doubt me because I'm little. Sometimes proving others wrong is the motivation we need to pick ourselves up and keep going. The more you believe you are capable of, the less people who tell you otherwise matter. We should set the bar higher for other people, too. Just because someone's little, different, sick, disabled, or anything else doesn't mean we shouldn't expect a lot from him or her. We should expect better from people who bully, too. We should expect everyone to be capable of kindness and empathy. People who bully don't get a free pass.

6. Don't be silent. Whether you're being bullied, know someone who is, or watch it happen, don't keep that information to yourself. Tell a teacher, a parent, a counselor, a friend, or anyone else you trust. I always thought that if I talked about being bullied at school I was a tattletale or a snitch, that if I told my parents or my teachers, it was me doing something wrong. But that's not true! You deserve to feel safe and to be respected, no matter what the bullies say.

We've all heard the old saying, "Sticks and stones may break my bones, but words can never hurt me." But that's just not true. Words can break your heart. Sometimes words hurt more than actions. They could be the tipping point for someone.

"No Offense...."
How to Tell When Teasing Has Gone Too Far:

- Someone stops showing up at school in order to avoid it.

- The same person is the only one ever teased for the same things.

- The people doing the teasing aren't actually friends or close with the person being teased.

- Teasing escalates into physical violence, threats, or relentless online comments.

You don't know what other people are going through, and something you think is a joke or harmless fun might be the thing that ruins someone's life. I thought "that video" was going to break me, but I surprised myself with the strength I was capable of (with the help of my support system). I had a choice to fight back for revenge and sink to the bullying level or choose to be happy and get strong with a good life and my accomplishments. God has given me a lot of milestones and even more boulders to overcome, but it's all been done to make me stronger.

To go back to the story I told at the beginning of this section, I know now I'm strong enough to survive whatever the bullies throw at me. It might still hurt, but it also provides me another opportunity to practice what I preach. None of us knows what's really going on in another person's life, and that includes the bullies we come across. That's why I don't hit my keyboard and fight back in a negative way. I don't want to be a bully. I don't want anyone to be hurt the way I was, even if—in the heat of the moment—it seems like they deserve it. So here are a few ways to respond positively to bullies, whether you meet in them in real life or online:

☆ Ignore them. If you're too upset to respond without getting angry, don't waste your time by responding.

☆ Tell them to stop staring and start learning.

☆ Pray for them. And not in a sarcastic way or in a "I-hope-they-get-what-they-deserve" way. Pray sincerely.

☆ Tell them you hope whatever's hurting in their life gets better.

☆ Unplug and walk away. When things start to get too heated on the internet (and trust me, I know), the only way you can keep from getting sucked in is to walk away for a while. Getting the last word in isn't worth it. I promise.

Reflect

Where do you see bullying in your life?

How can you help make things better?

Make an action plan on how you can improve your corner of the world (or the internet).

Make a list of ways you can use social media for good.

Go Out and Live It!

One negative comment can be enough to push someone over the edge, but one positive comment can be enough to pull that person back. Post something nice today. No matter what social media you use, or somewhere else, let someone know today you think he or she is awesome.

CHAPTER 4

Friendships and Relationships — Waiting for the Right One(s)

> *Two are better than one: They get a good wage for their toil. If the one falls, the other will help the fallen one. But woe to the solitary person! If that one should fall, there is no other to help.*
>
> ECCLESIASTES 4:9–10

Friends for Life

There are friends who bring ruin, but there are true friends more loyal than a brother.

PROVERBS 18:24

ating alone at the lunch table, staying in on a Friday night, never being in a relationship, or never having someone to share your secrets with are all legitimate fears that each and every one of us has had in some way. My fears were all of the above, plus I was afraid no one would be able to look past my appearance and see me for who I am. It took a while for me to find my niche with my group of friends, but eventually I found myself surrounded with awesome, supportive people. All the memories, the hours spent on the phone, the giggling, and even the crying all joined together as the ingredients we needed to form a solid foundation of friendship.

When I would make a friend, at first I would unconsciously stick to that person like glue. In my mind, I had made an awesome friend, so the worries and fears of having to make other friends went out the window. As long as I had that one person, that one friend, I didn't need to venture out into the rest of the world and take a risk on anyone else. In fact, when I was younger, my friends acted like my bodyguards. They were the people who vouched for me with the other kids, letting them know that even though I looked different, I was still like them.

It's very surreal for me to think that I used to pray at night that God would not only change my appearance but that he would also send me friends. I wanted to have friends like in the movies.

I imagined having the best sleep-overs, staying up super-late eating junk food, dancing, and singing at the top of our lungs, watching movie after movie, and all those other picture-perfect things friends seem to do in movies and on TV. But in real life, sometimes our friendships look different. We might have sleep-overs with some friends, go to soccer practice with others, and hang out at school with a combination of all of them. Looking back, I now realize I have three very distinct groups of friends. I truly believe each one of them was put into my life for a reason. These weren't just people I could confide in. They were people who could teach me in so many ways and about so many things.

My first real group of friends was established when I was just a six-month-old, wide-eyed, curly haired girl. At the time, my mom had to quit her job to stay home with me. In hopes of raising me just like a normal child, my mom thought it would be a good idea to baby-sit a couple of kids during the day so I could learn the basic skills of being around other kids. One of those skills was sharing toys, which, according to my mom, wasn't a skill I was too fond of. Nikki, my cousin, and Angelica, whom I called Jelly, were my first two best friends in the world. I was a lot smaller than they were, but if you watched our old home videos, you'd be shocked at how bossy I was! If one of them wanted to play with a toy I had, I would get so bothered and then give them a specific time when they could use it. Looking back on those instances, I know none of us had a clue what time actually meant, but Nikki and Jelly would always agree with me.

My mom watched Nikki and Jelly up until we were all in middle school. It was sad when we started middle school because we were all going somewhere different, which meant we had to get used to not being together all the time. It was very strange not having my two musketeers by my side. Every year we would look forward to summertime because that meant they would both come to my house every day, and my mom would always have the best activities for us to do. Looking back, I laugh because I remember the night before the girls would get to our house I would set up the different centers around the living room and I'd have a schedule for them to follow. Who was I? I'm sure glad they liked me even with my bossy side!

The three of us went through so many different phases together. There was the Power Rangers phase, where Jelly and I would have huge fights about who was going to be the Pink Ranger. There was the 'N Sync phase, where we would dream about members of the band and always beg our parents to take us to one of their concerts. My two personal favorite phases were our Harriet the Spy phase and our Spice Girls phase. We watched the Harriet movie and the one with the Spice Girls so many times that my mom eventually had to hide the VHS tapes from us. The three of us would spend hours in front of the TV studying how to be just like the Spice Girls. We bought clothes like the Spice Girls and worked on memorizing the songs and choreographed dance moves so we could be a girl band of our own. Then when we weren't too busy being the newest pop sensation, we had our cool composition books and dark ink pens we used to spy on our parents, just like Harriet.

I am beyond thankful for every friendship I've ever had, but these two by far have a special place in my heart. One of the things that I adore about my friendships with them is that during the entire time growing up, we never talked about my syndrome. It never came up in conversation, and they never expressed curiosity about why I looked different. To them I was just Lizzie. I wouldn't change that for the world. Because I was blessed to have friends like this at the beginning of my life, I could go out into the world confident that, when the time came to make new friends, my syndrome wasn't going to be a factor. If there were already two people in my life who could see past my syndrome, I knew there would be more. There were still days I had my doubts, but having my two best friends to turn to made life a lot easier to handle.

Choosing to Take Chances

I was lucky to have made good friends so early, but I still had my fair share of time spent alone. In elementary school, the other kids were scared of me because I looked so different. It took a lot of courage to go up and ask to play with them anyway. I got used to being isolated and left out of groups, but I can almost understand it. Little kids always stare at things that look different. They aren't sure how to react to them. It hurt, but not as much as when I got older. Middle school was the worst. People would point and whisper about me to their friends. They were mean on purpose. It wasn't because they didn't understand me, it was because they didn't want to. I felt not only alone, but abandoned. I wanted someone to blame.

But blaming other people didn't help me make new friends, it just made me alone and angry. I decided to start taking chances by joining clubs and introducing myself to other people. I spent a lot of time praying, begging that God would send me friends. As I got older and more confident, I started to find people who treated me like everyone else. I joined every club I could find. I took pictures for yearbook even though I am blind in one eye and joined the drama club even though I hate acting (I even won an award!). Once people started to see I was just like them, it became easier to make friends. People were willing to open up to me, and once people knew me and my story, the pointing and whispering didn't happen as much. Things weren't perfect, but they were a lot better!

There are a lot of reasons you or someone you know might feel alone. You might have been bullied by your classmates, like me, you might be the new kid at school, you might be the only one of your friends to go to a certain college, or you might have had to move away from all your friends and family for your first job. It can be really depressing to feel like you're the only one, but if me and Nikki and Angelica had all gone to the same school, I might never have had to branch out and learn how strong I could be. I might have missed out on some of the amazing things I've done with some amazing new people. If I'd known more people going to my college, I might never have had to step outside my comfort zone and make new college friends.

But feeling alone is sometimes more complicated than just leaving your old friends behind and starting something new. In fact, this can be the easiest kind of alone to fix. I'm a people person. Even without my old friends with me, I like to be around people and have no problem going up to someone and introducing myself. But sometimes I've felt alone for other reasons, even when surrounded by my friends. Obviously, my syndrome is a big part of that. I felt alone because I was the only person I knew who had this syndrome. I didn't think anyone would be able to relate to anything I was going through. I felt alone because I felt different. I wanted to be part of something but felt like my syndrome would always keep me from really being included.

Once I started to speak about it, though, I started to realize I wasn't as alone as I thought. There may only be two other people in the world with a syndrome like mine, but everyone has gone through some of what I have in his or her own way.

- How many of you have ever looked in the mirror and wished for a different face ?

- How many of you have felt excluded from groups ?

- How many of you have felt guys (or girls) would never be able to see you as relationship material ?

- How many of you have ever been scared about the future ?

- How many of you have ever been called names or made fun of ?

I'll bet every one of you is able to say "yes" to at least one of these questions, if not all of them, which means none of us is really as alone as we think.

Instead of keeping to yourself, look for someone else eating by herself or sitting alone. Say hi! Sign up for a club you're interested in and see who else shares that same passion. Ask to join a group at lunch. You'll be surprised how often the answer is "yes!" And if it's not? Then those are the people you don't want to be hanging out with anyway. If you still need a boost in confidence, call up old friends who already think you're amazing. Talk to them about how you feel. Remind yourself they're still there.

And when you do find that awesome group of new friends, don't forget to keep in touch with the old ones. In middle school, I was split from my two best friends. In college, I had to start over completely, and now I'm on the road a lot and feel like I never have a chance to be at home! All of these things make it hard to keep those old friendships healthy. I'm just too busy! But that's a really bad excuse for not keeping in touch. Even if it's just a couple of times a month, take your friendships offline and make a phone call or set a lunch date. Go out and catch up. Make the effort. It's easy to think we're so busy that our old friends should get in touch with us. We don't have time to pick up the phone and call, but, for some reason, we assume they do. Don't fall into this trap! Real friendships aren't about what people can or should be doing for you. They're about what we do for each other. It's another place in our life where we have to choose. We can choose to lose friends and be bitter no one is calling us up, or we can choose to be positive and reach out to them.

Being Honest

But whether it happens in middle school, high school, college, or even later in life, we all lose friends. Sometimes for good reasons and sometimes over stupid stuff. The important thing to remember is that trying to put all the blame on someone else is never useful. Bad things happen, friendships end, but that doesn't wipe out all the good things. You can treasure all the inside jokes and unforgettable moments without being filled with rage that the other person messed everything up. In fact, some of these things may actually help you save a good friendship that's starting to fall apart. So if you're starting to feel you and a friend are growing apart but not for any of the reasons listed in the previous section, here are a few things you can do to try and save the friendship or walk away on good terms:

1. **Own up to your mistakes.**

   Have you done something wrong that's creating tension in your friendship? Be willing to say so. Apologize before things get worse and let your friend know it won't happen in the future. If she's really your friend she'll be willing to accept a sincere apology and move on. In fact, that's probably all she wants.

2. **Be willing to forgive.**

   This is the other side of No. 1. If your friend is really sorry, be willing to accept that apology, talk about things, and move on. This doesn't mean being a doormat! If someone consistently treats you badly or acts like your feelings are less important than his, it's time to cut him out of your life.

3. **Talk to your friend.**

   If your friend is doing something that upsets you and she doesn't stop or apologize, be brave and start the conversation. Don't expect her to come to you. She might not even realize that what she's doing bothers you. Being willing to talk about things before they've gone too far is one way to keep from having a friendship end in a fight.

4. Listen to outsiders.

Sometimes other friends and family members might be able to see a bad friendship before you can. It's easier for them because they aren't blinded by all those good times. They can see how our friends change and, more importantly, how we change around our friends. If someone tells you he's concerned about you in this friendship/relationship, it's time to take a step back and look at whether or not you're your best self with this person or group.

5. Don't do things you aren't comfortable with.

When I started to lose friends just because one person decided the friendship wasn't worthwhile, I was a little uncomfortable. These friends had been nice to me, and I didn't see anything wrong with them. But I didn't do anything about it at the time. Whether it's isolating yourself or something else your friend is doing that makes you uncomfortable, be brave and speak up. If she isn't willing to listen to you, it's probably not a healthy friendship.

It takes two people for any friendship to work. And just like a relationship with your significant other, if one person in the relationship is putting in all the effort, the friendship is going to fall apart. Be willing to admit your mistakes, be willing to talk, and be willing to make the effort. If the other person isn't willing to work with you, it's time to let the friendship go.

Reflect

Who are the people in my life I can't live without?

Have I made an effort to keep in touch with old friends?

Have I ever seen someone by herself who looks like she could use a friend?

Have I tried to get to know her or include her in my circle?

Go Out and Do It!

① Step outside of your comfort zone this week and sign up for something you've always wanted to do, even if it means going alone and meeting new people.

② If you have an old friend you haven't talked to in a while, get in touch. Set a time to go out and catch up.

Knowing When to Wait

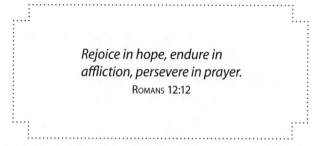

Rejoice in hope, endure in affliction, persevere in prayer.
Romans 12:12

One question I'm asked all the time (especially by my awesome followers) is whether I have a boyfriend. The answer is no. Not right now, but boy do I have stories. You would not even believe! Right after my TED talk went viral, I got texts from three guys I'd liked in the past but hadn't heard from in months (years for some of them). The first thing I texted back was, "Why now?" and if their answer wasn't genuine, big red flags started showing up.

Why?

Because someone who doesn't really want to be with you but is enchanted with just the idea of you or the things he thinks he can get from you is not worth the time. From the beginning, it's a relationship doomed to fail. And why would you want that?

When I was younger (well, in high school), I really wanted to be appreciated by a guy. My friends were starting to get boyfriends, or guys in our class were noticing them, and I wanted that. I wanted the attention. I wanted to know somebody cared about me "in that way." I thought that if I could get a boyfriend or if guys would start getting crushes on me, it meant I fit in. It was another aspect of my life where I thought if things could just go how I wanted them to, I wouldn't be so different. It would mean I belonged. Not having a guy in my life when my friends did was depressing. I thought it meant I didn't deserve that kind of love. I thought it meant there was something wrong with me, that this was one part of my life where I couldn't just be strong and get through. But I can finally say (and trust me, it's taken a lot to get to this point), underneath it all, the one big reason I wanted that kind of love was because I couldn't do it myself. I couldn't love and appreciate myself, and I thought I needed a guy to do that for me.

Struggling to get guys to notice me was hard, as all girls who have ever struggled to be noticed by a guy in high school can commiserate about. For me though, there has always been an extra step, and it's that extra step that made it even harder to convince myself I deserved love, that I was even lovable at all in that way. For normal teen relationships, the biggest hurdle in the beginning is getting a guy to notice you and making sure that the guy likes you the way you like him. It's messy, it's complicated, and there are days we wonder if it's worth it. Well for me, that's hurdle two. Hurdle one is getting the guy to realize I'm normal, to get past the way my syndrome makes me look and see me for who I am. And that's a pretty tall hurdle for a high-school kid.

It's taken a lot of prayer, soul searching, and growing up for me to realize that loving and appreciating myself is something I'm capable of. Not being in a relationship doesn't mean you're any less worthy of love than your friend who is. And just because you've been single for a long time doesn't mean you should just settle for any guy who comes along and says he likes you. It's taken me a few years of observing other people's relationships and experiencing some of my own to realize trying to make something work just because you want to be "in a relationship" is a waste of time, and people usually end up getting hurt.

Choosing the Right Time

I want to let you in on a secret. It's a secret I wish someone had told me instead of letting me spend so much time feeling broken and anxious (although if I hadn't come to the conclusion myself, I probably wouldn't have believed it). Work on yourself first. We should all spend less time waiting for the right guy and devote more time waiting for the right time. I spent so many nights wishing for the right guy to come along the next day that I ignored everything else I had. I would send God my wish list but wouldn't listen for his response. I wouldn't wait around to hear him saying it isn't time yet, or I'd ignore him completely.

But then I did start working on myself. I started loving and appreciating myself. I started working toward being the kind of person I want to be when it is time to meet Mr. Right. I'm excited to know God is working on the right guy for me, and I'm willing to wait and be single as long as it takes for someone that awesome. And while I've been waiting, I've realized that God is working to make me even more awesome, too. I'm also starting to ask myself some tough questions I think we should all ask before jumping into a relationship:

- Is this the right time for me to be in a relationship? There are days I want a relationship because my friends have them, and I think, I want that, too. But just because it's the right time for someone else doesn't mean it's the right time for you. I'm happy being single. Right now, I am my first priority, and that's OK!

- Is it the right time for Mr. or Ms. Right? Wouldn't you rather be in a relationship with someone who has put time in to work on himself and is confident in who he is than someone who expects you to do that work for him? The right person is worth waiting for. Don't settle for the wrong one.

- Would I be able to devote myself and my time to the kind of relationship I want? Be honest with yourself. What is your first priority? If you're in high school and your first priority is getting into a good college, that doesn't mean you can't date or have a boyfriend or girlfriend, but it does mean you shouldn't have the same kind of relationship as someone who is looking to get married and whose priority is finding a spouse.

- Would it be fair to another person to be in a relationship right now? Are my real priorities school, my job, finding out more about myself? If you're in a relationship just to be in one but don't actually have any time to spend with your other half—and aren't willing to make time—you need to either reprioritize or take a step back.

- Do I want a significant other because I can't love myself alone? If you just want a relationship because you can't love yourself, you shouldn't be in one. Don't sacrifice getting to know yourself, loving yourself, and being confident in who you are for letting someone else tell you. This is probably the hardest reason to stay single, but it has the biggest reward.

- Is this what I want or what my friends want? If the only good reason you can think of to be in a relationship is that your friends are in one, take some time to figure out what you want. If you find out you actually want to be single, that's OK. There's nothing wrong with you.

After I answered these questions for myself, I came to some tough but ultimately liberating conclusions. I still want someone to love in my life, and I want my own family...eventually, but not right now. I'm totally devoted to my mission. I want to speak and write and explore my opportunities to expand my message, and right now that's taking up 110 percent of my time. I don't have the time to devote to the kind of relationship I eventually want to have. I'd be asking a guy to put 100 percent into our future and our relationship, but I wouldn't be able to do that myself. Is that how I want to treat Mr. Right?

It's hard to see my friends get married and have children while I'm still single, but it also helps to reinforce that I'm not ready yet. I don't really have anything to complain about. I don't want to rush into something and have regrets. We all have to make the decision that's right for us. It can be hard—especially if you're still in middle school or high school—to make that decision when it seems like the only thing anyone cares about is whether or not you're dating someone. It gets even harder when you start to think the reason you're single is that you aren't as good as your friends, that you aren't attractive enough or special enough to get a guy's or a girl's attention. But that's not true. Just like I'm excited to meet the awesome guy God has planned for me, you should be excited to meet the right guy or girl for you. In the meantime, enjoy being single! Enjoy figuring out who you are and trying new things. There's no reason to sit home alone and wait.

Reflect

Do I want to settle for just any relationship or wait for the right one?

What is my main priority during this stage of my life? Why?

What relationships am I using as models for my own?

How does my current relationship fit in with my plans for the future?

Go Out and Do It!

Whether you're single, dating, or married, take time this week to do something just for yourself. Don't lose sight of your goals as an individual just because you want someone to share them with.

CHAPTER 5

Inspiration —
Choosing to Be Happy

> I have told you this so that you might
> have peace in me. In the world you
> will have trouble, but take courage,
> I have conquered the world.
>
> JOHN 16:33

It's Just How I Was Raised

> *Train the young in the way they should go; even when old, they will not swerve from it.*
>
> Proverbs 22:6

One of the things I talked about in the bullying section was having a strong support system. I'd like to take this opportunity to expand on that. Whatever success I have achieved today isn't just because of me. God knew what he was doing when he sent me to my parents. I can only imagine how scary it was for them, as first-time parents, to have a baby like me. When I was born, the doctors told them I'd never be able to do anything on my own. I wouldn't be able to walk, I wouldn't be able to talk, I wouldn't be able to have any kind of normal life. But my parents kept me anyway. They said they were going to take me home, love me, and raise me as well as they could.

My parents raised me beautifully. I've never weighed more than sixty-four pounds, and as a baby I was the size of a doll. Regular baby clothes didn't fit me, so my parents got creative. They dressed me in Cabbage Patch Kids doll clothes, which worked out even better than they could have imagined, because once I got older I got to use all those clothes for my dolls! In addition to being hard to dress, I also got sick a lot because I have a weak immune system. I've never liked to rest, so my parents had to work to keep me healthy. They never kept me cut off from the world, though. I always had friends or cousins over to play with, and everyone treated me normally. I was never pitied or treated like I'd break if I did what other kids did, and I think that helped me enter the world of "normal" even with my syndrome.

Once I got to school, things got more complicated. I was no longer surrounded by people who knew me as just Lizzie. The other kids didn't know what to think of me, and more often than not, they were scared of me. When the day finally came for me to ask my parents why I was different, they had their answer ready to go, and I credit a lot of who I am to this moment. My parents sat me down and explained my syndrome to me. They didn't have one negative word to say to me. They never said, "You'll never be able to..." or, "you're not like the other kids because..." or, "you can't...." All they said was, "You were born with this syndrome, but you're just like everyone else. You look different, but that doesn't mean you aren't like any other kid."

When I asked my parents how I was going to go back to school when the other kids didn't want to play with me or laughed at me or were scared of me, they told me to walk into the classroom with my chin up and a smile on my face. If I acted like there was nothing wrong with me and showed the other kids how much fun I was to be around, eventually they'd see me the way I saw myself. It wasn't easy, but I got the strength I needed to keep going back to school, and eventually things started to get better.

Choose Your Role Models

If I had had different parents, I don't think I'd be the same person I am today. They have influenced my personality and the way I react to situations. They raised me like a normal kid, in spite of my syndrome. When my brother and sister were born, they treated us all the same. They didn't have one set of rules for Lizzie and one set of rules for everyone else. No one was more or less important than anyone else. We were all family. They kept us all grounded in our faith and taught us to treat everyone with kindness and respect, even when it was difficult.

I learned a lot of little things from them, too, things I'm not even sure they intentionally meant to teach me. My parents never sat me down and told me these were the values and morals I had to learn and use for the rest of my life, I just learned from watching how they reacted to things. Shortly before I started writing this book, my mom got really sick because of a mistake the people at the hospital made during a routine surgery. People kept asking my dad if he was going to sue, but he just shook his head, saying all we wanted to do at the moment was get my mom better.

That is not how I would have responded. I would have been on the phone with a lawyer immediately. I wanted to make someone pay. But by doing that, I'd be ignoring my mom, the person who actually was hurting and in need of support. That person should always come first. Family should come first.

If it weren't for my parents, I also wouldn't have my sense of humor. It's taken a long time and a lot of struggling to be able to laugh about my syndrome and the bullying. My parents have always said that whenever anything bad happens you get one good cry and then you have to move on. You can't spend the rest of your life feeling sorry for yourself. Without being able to laugh at myself, I don't think I'd be the same person. If I took everything about my situation too seriously, I'd probably never have the strength to get out of bed, and I certainly wouldn't be inspiring people to choose happiness for themselves.

The last and maybe most important thing I learned from my parents is my faith. I don't know any other way. My walk with God has actually been more like riding a roller coaster. I've always believed God was there, but I didn't always like him. When I was struggling to come to terms with my syndrome, I wanted someone to blame, so I blamed God. I hated him for not answering my prayers and giving me a normal face. It has not been easy to go from seeing this syndrome as a curse to seeing it as a blessing. Once I did, things really didn't get easier, but I no longer felt like I was struggling alone. Any time I want to talk to God, I know he's there. It's become second nature that when I'm on my knees I can just surrender everything to God. Being able to offer it up has been a huge gift. Without it, I don't think I'd have the strength to be here today. My faith is what keeps me going.

Choose Your Inspiration

I know I'm lucky to have the parents I have; I'm lucky they've been such a positive influence on me. But not everyone is as lucky as me. Some of you might have to look a little further for a role model, or you might be in the position of trying to be a role model for someone else but aren't sure where to start. Here are a few things I've learned from watching my parents that might give you a place to start:

♥ Be positive

If someone is being bullied, he's getting enough negative feedback to last a lifetime. If she's a teenage girl (like I was), she's probably already good at picking out what's wrong with her. It's easy to see the bad things. It's hard to see the good things in front of you. Focus on those. Role models should make the path to choosing happiness more clear. They might not be able to make it easier, but if they start to make you feel hopeless, it's time to find others to look up to.

💜 Listen

When I was in middle school and high school, I was trying to figure out who I was, trying to come to terms with my syndrome, wondering why boys didn't like me, learning some hard-to-stomach truths about the real world, and countless other things I thought would be the end of the world. That's a lot going on. I needed to talk, but more than that I needed to be taken seriously. Looking back, I may have slightly overreacted to some things, but I didn't need to be told that at the time. Sometimes all you need is someone to hear you out, and sometimes all you need to do is be open to listening without offering an opinion.

💜 Be comfortable

The best conversations I've had with my parents didn't take place under interrogation. They happened spontaneously in the car while we were going somewhere or over dinner, places I felt like I could open up without all the attention being on me. Places I felt safe. Sitting down and saying, "Let's talk about your feelings" never worked for me. It's a little intimidating, too. Part of being a good listener is letting someone come to you on his or her own terms.

💜 Be supportive

This doesn't mean your role model should support you doing something that might cause you harm, but if you have a dream or goal that seems a little out of reach, talk about how to get there. Don't write it off as impossible. No one in my family had any idea how to start a motivational-speaking/writing career, but no one tried to stop me from trying, either.

We all need someone to talk to no matter how strong we are, and having someone to look up to and get advice from makes the journey a lot easier. Be brave enough to ask someone for help or advice. If you aren't sure you're ready to take that step yet, or if you're afraid to let someone know there's something going on (it took me a lot of private reflection before I was ready to tell my parents I was being bullied), or if you want to be the kind of person someone could look up to but aren't sure you're confident enough in yourself yet, you still have some options. I chose to pray. Talking to God, even when I was yelling at God, helped me. Knowing there was always someone to talk to—no matter what I was going through or where I was—helped. If you're not quite there yet in your own relationship with God, or you're not even sure if you believe in God, that's OK.

I've also found journaling to be a big help while struggling to work things out for myself. Write whatever you want. You can write about your future, your dreams, your nightmares, your struggles, or just something that makes you happy.

If writing doesn't appeal to you, listen to music. I have a "get happy" mix for days when I'm feeling down or when I've gotten nasty emails or comments from people. The music doesn't keep the bad things from happening, but it does make them easier to get through.

Reflect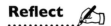

Who are the people you look up to? These can include people you haven't met in person but admire anyway.

Why do you look up to the people you listed in No. 1?

If someone said she looked up to you, what would you want her to see?

What are things you can do to make a bad day better? Make a list and then put it someplace where you'll see it when you're having a bad day.

Go Out and Live It!

Take time today to thank someone who inspires you to choose happiness. It can be in an email, a post somewhere, a handwritten note, or just a quick conversation in person or over the phone. Whether it's a parent, a teacher, a friend, a sibling, a relative, a blogger, a writer, a child, or anyone else: Let that person know. Knowing how much you care might help that person choose happiness in the future, too.

Inspiring Social Media

> *We must consider how to rouse one another to love and good works. We should not stay away from our assembly, as is the custom of some, but encourage one another....*
>
> HEBREWS 10:24–25

I have had bad experiences with social media. In fact, you could say a bad experience with social media is what made me who I am. But I also don't want people to get the idea that the internet is all bad. The cyber-bullies and trolls who hide behind usernames and attack other people are just a small fraction of the people you can meet on the internet. Actually you can meet some pretty inspiring people online, people who can help you choose happiness on your darkest days, because they've had pretty dark days, too.

There are so many people who inspire me online, I couldn't hope to name them all, so I've chosen a few of the people I've been following recently to show you how other people in the world are choosing happiness, too.

I Am That Girl

You might have the name Alexis Jones on your mind because she was kind enough to write the foreword for this book. But she's more than just my foreword writer. She is my inspiration. Alexis started the I Am That Girl organization to turn self-doubt into self-love. The internet can be a dark and depressing place (as we've already established), but Alexis Jones and everyone else involved in the IATG project are making it a little bit brighter every day. They are choosing happiness by choosing to be themselves and by choosing to tell other girls it's OK to be weird, look different than "normal," and go out and take good risks.

This whole project inspires me to choose happiness for a lot of the same reasons. Choosing to be different is hard, especially when you don't have a choice. Some of us have been born with the things that will cause us to get singled out in life. We don't choose our skin color. We don't choose whether society will consider us beautiful when we grow up. We don't choose how much money our family has. We don't choose the parents we're born to. We don't choose how other people will decide to see us. But we can choose to try and change what we don't like. We can choose to love ourselves the way we are. We can choose to not judge people. We can choose to try and make a difference.

Alexis and her team saw something they wanted to change and found a way to get change started. I would love to expand my message into a project like that. I actually plan to start something in the future. Whenever keeping my message out there seems too hard, or the speaking engagements are too exhausting, the book writing is too much work, or responding to all the emails I get is just too much, I look to Alexis and see ways to make possible the things that seem impossible. I can do it all if I choose to, if I prioritize and organize, if I delegate and create a team. I am that girl.

Adalia Rose

Adalia Rose Williams makes me feel guilty about ever choosing anything but happiness. Adalia is a seven-year-old girl with progeria (a rare disease that dramatically speeds up the aging process). She is full of only the good things in life, and any time I need to remind myself why it's so important to choose happiness, I just need to look at her. This little girl is a diva! She sings, dances, dresses up, and spreads happiness to anyone who sees her.

If I dressed up like a princess and started to dance in my Vlogs like she does, it might not be fun in the same way, but I'm still inspired by everything Adalia Rose does. She inspires me to choose happiness because there's so much to be happy about! So what if I have this syndrome that keeps me from living the same kind of life I might have had otherwise. I can still sing along to my iPod, I can still dance around with my friends, I can eat any and all of my favorite foods whenever I want and not feel guilty. I can use my disease to help other people choose to be happy. It doesn't always have to be choosing happiness to overcome some obstacle in your path or rise above someone's mean comment. It can be about choosing happiness just because you can.

I wish we could all be more like Adalia Rose. Just embracing life, loving what we love, and not having to worry about what other people might think.

You!

I choose happiness for and because of all of you. Whether you're a longtime fan or this book is the first time you've heard of Lizzie Velasquez, I choose happiness for myself because of you. When my parents had me, they had a tough choice to make. They could have easily chosen to feel sorry for themselves and wail about why God would give them and their daughter such a hardship to overcome. But they rejected that path. They chose happiness and taught me how to do the same for myself. I could feel sorry for myself every day, but then I wouldn't be able to help any of you.

I once received a video message from a follower. She had just watched my TED talk and said it brought her to tears. A few days before, her cousin had committed suicide. She said if he had seen my TED talk, it might have changed his mind. She told me how important my message was, how much it had helped her. I was in tears before the message was over. You might think messages like these help boost my confidence in myself, make me feel like such a great speaker and writer. But they don't. These messages are the most humbling experience I can imagine. They are a reminder that I am not doing this for myself anymore. I'm doing this for all of you.

I choose happiness so I can help other people do the same, and all of you I've interacted with in person or online help me to continue to make that choice.

Choose to Inspire

You don't need to have a disease, syndrome, or anything else to go out and be an inspiration yourself. There are no qualifications to be an inspiration for someone else. You can just go out and do it. Sometimes inspiring other people can be as simple as choosing to be happy for yourself and not hiding that happiness from others. Sometimes it can happen when you stand up for someone else and set an example.

One of the things I'd really like to work to make happen is getting people to use social media to make positive changes. I've been really hurt by social media, and people still use it to lash out at me and others to make people feel bad about themselves. Changing all those people is impossible, but changing how we react to them and with each other isn't. My challenge to all of you reading this book is to go out and be an inspiration online. Here are some ways you can do that:

✳ Keep posting positive

Stay away from retweeting, blogging, or passing on celebrity gossip or other stories of people behaving badly. Instead, pass on stories of people spreading happiness to others or making the choice to be happy themselves.

✳ Leave encouraging comments

Don't jump into an online fight when you see one breaking out in the comments section. Say something positive if you can, but if you can't, don't post at all. Walk away from your cell phone, tablet, or computer for five minutes—longer, if you have to.

✳ Share your own choosing-happiness story

I know I can't be the only one who struggles to choose happiness! Let others know your choosing-happiness story, and let them know joy is possible.

Reflect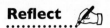

What inspires you to choose happiness?

Who are the people you choose happiness for?

What makes you happy when you're about to give up?

Make a list of ways you could inspire someone else to choose happiness.

Go Out and Do It!

Choose to be happy. Make time for what makes you happy. Pick something off your list in No. 4 and give it a try sometime this week.

Conclusion

When I started down the path that led me to this unbelievable life I'm living now, I had five goals:

1. Become a professional motivational speaker.
2. Write a book.
3. Graduate from college.
4. Be in control of my own career.
5. Start my own family.

As of today, I have been a motivational speaker for almost eight years. This is my third book. I graduated from college with a degree in communication studies and a minor in English. I am taking my career to a new level. As for the family, well that's a little further down the road. But I'm not done yet.

Those goals were just the beginning. They were the goals that got me started. My next set of goals is even bigger. I'm ready to move past "that video," and I think I'm finally in a position to do that. I have used all that publicity to start changing my message, I've drawn people in, and it's served its purpose. I no longer have to be "the world's ugliest woman" or "the girl labeled as the world's ugliest woman." I can move forward with my message as just Lizzie Velasquez. In fact, I have some pretty big things coming up in the next year, things that might be the biggest I've ever had the opportunity to be a part of….And you'll have to keep following me to see exactly what they are!

I'm not sure what that message is going to be yet. There are so many people I'm touching with my mission right now, I don't want to change it, but I do want to make it bigger. I see myself starting my own company to support people going through hard times and in need of a supporting community. I love computers, graphic design, and making websites, and I'd like to grow my skills in those areas and find a way to use them toward fulfilling my mission.

If I had to say something about the future of my mission, I'd say it's going to focus on answering the many facets of these three questions:

What is happiness?

What is beauty?

What is success?

Society hands us definitions of these terms, and many of us think those are the only definitions we have to go on. I disagree. I believe we make our own definitions of happiness, beauty, and success. I believe we start making our definitions when we start figuring out who we are and what's important to us. We can do that in two ways: listening to what other people label us and assuming that's all we can hope to be, or throwing those labels away and seeing what we're capable of as who we are.

I know how hard it can be to get rid of labels. I'm still working on it myself, but I know choosing happiness is the first step. If we can take the bad labels people give us—along with the doubt and the limitations those labels bring with them, be happy, use the doubt for motivation, and our accomplishments to make us satisfied—we are one step closer to living a happy, joyous life. I hope the stories and reflections you've seen throughout the book will help you on your journey. Choosing happiness isn't just something you do once and check off your list. You have to make that choice every day.

Some days you won't be happy. That happens to me. But never give up. Never.

If you ever find yourself wondering how you can keep choosing happiness, if that choice feels like one you can't make on your own, go back through your journal pages here and remind yourself what your goal is. Remind yourself who you are choosing happiness for and why. Take a look at your list of inspirational people and go to them for help. Reach out to your role models, friends, family, and God. You are not alone. You are capable of truly awesome things. No one has the right to hold you back.

Even if I never meet you in person, I want you to know I will keep you in my thoughts and prayers every day. We are making the choice to choose happiness together!

Sincerely,

Lizzie Velasquez

Resources

Bullying Prevention

stopbullying.gov: If you're a parent or teacher who sees bullying going on online or in other ways, this website offers ways you can keep it from getting worse and resources to help the person being bullied. It also gives a list of warning signs to tell if someone is being bullied or is a bully. Stop it before it starts.

bullyingpreventioninstitute.org: The Highmark Foundation offers resources for parents and teachers to stay educated on the topic of bullying prevention and is working to help make schools bullying free.

pacer.org: Pacer provides resources for parents and teachers as well as kids in school. Its We Will Generation program promotes students as the catalysts to changing the attitude toward bullying in schools.

1-800-273-TALK (8255): The National Suicide Prevention Lifeline provides 24/7 crisis counseling and can refer you to a nearby counselor if you start to feel things will never get better.

Online Communities and Inspiration

iamthatgirl.com
This movement inspires girls to be, love, and express who they are. On the site you can find blog posts and videos to help you become That Girl, plus some fun, inspirational quotes and pictures on the site's inspiration page. If you want to take the inspiration out into the world, you can create a local chapter with girls in your community.

onebillionrising.org
This community asks women survivors of violence—physical or emotional—to step out and tell their story in an attempt to get justice and increase awareness. You can find an event in your area. Organize one! Just look through the group's resources to get you started.

adaliarose.com
I mentioned her as one of my big inspirations for choosing happiness. If you need a pick-me-up today, go to her website, read her story, and watch some of her videos. You'll be happier for it!

ted.com
This website offers you more than 1,700 TED talks to get you inspired about whatever it is you want to be inspired to do.

Lizzie Velasquez is a graduate of Texas State University in San Marcos. She is one of three known people in the world with a medical syndrome that doesn't allow her to gain weight. Lizzie has appeared as a motivational speaker at more than 200 events, including the TEDxAustin event in 2013. Her story has been featured nationally and internationally, including on *Today*, *The View*, *E! News*, *Inside Edition*, Katie Couric's and Dr. Drew's talk shows, *Sunday Night* in Australia, and *Explosiv* in Germany. A television documentary about Lizzie is planned. This is her third book. She is partnering with I Am That Girl and Women Rising to create and produce media for motivating, empowering, and connecting women.

More About Lizzie!

To find out more about Lizzie and to contact her for a speaking engagement, visit her online in several places:

- Lizzie's website: aboutlizzie.com
- YouTube: youtube.com/user/lizzitachickita
- Twitter: @littlelizziev
- Facebook: Facebook.com/LizzieVelasquez